M000034654

DOG TRAINING BOOKS: GOLDEN RETRIEVER

Training Your Dog within 5 Weeks Using the Power of Positive Reinforcement (Golder Retriever Edition)

TABLE OF CONTENTS

INTRODUCTION

First, I want to thank you for purchasing my book "Dog Training Books Golden Retriever: Training Your Dog within 5 Weeks Using the Power of Positive Reinforcement (Golden Retriever Edition)". This book contains dog training steps and strategies that truly work.

Golden retrievers are smart, kind, playful creatures that adore their owners. Despite all the love they have to offer and happiness they introduce to our lives these dogs still need to be trained. Proper dog training is necessary to make sure your dog is happy and healthy, but also well-adjusted and well-behaved.

Many dog owners believe they can't train their dog. It's too tricky, the dog will hate them later, and what not. Let me tell you one thing: none of that is true! Sure, dog training is a demanding process regardless of breed, and golden retrievers are no exception. Although demanding, the whole process is incredibly rewarding because it allows you to bond and establish a deeper connection with your four-legged family member.

If it's a golden retriever, regardless of whether it's a puppy or an adult dog, and you wonder how to train him (or her), this book is perfect for you. Throughout this book, you'll learn more about golden retrievers and their character, which will help you to understand their needs and training process in general.

This book also explains the importance of positive reinforcement in dog training, provides a five-week schedule to train your dog, contains a list of useful and cool tricks to teach your golden retriever, and names all the useful things you should learn before you start training your pet.

In other words, this book is a wonderful source of informative and practical content that every golden retriever owner needs to know. Are you ready to embark on a journey with your beloved dog? Let's start, shall we?

CHAPTER 1:

1:
GROWTH, DEVELOPMENT, AND BEHAVIOR OF GOLDEN RETRIEVERS

This is not one of those books where you'll get complicated tips about dog training and nothing else. My goal is to provide a useful insight into golden retriever training using the same methods I used to train my dog, but also teach you about this breed. Golden retrievers are truly remarkable dogs, amazing pets, and irreplaceable family members. It's definitely worth learning a thing or two about them first. The more you know, the easier it is to understand your dog and adjust training in a manner best suited to your four-legged buddy. The very first chapter of this book provides breed information as well as info about growth, development, and behavior. So, let's start.

BREED OVERVIEW

One of the most popular dog breeds in the world, golden retrievers have a fascinating history. The golden retriever is a sturdy, muscular, medium-sized dog well-known for its dense, lustrous coat of gold, hence the name. Dogs from this breed have a broad head, friendly, warm, and intelligent eyes, short ears, and a straight muzzle. They are soft and kind creatures that move with a smooth yet powerful gait.

(Photo credit: Wikimedia Commons)

Have you ever wondered where golden retrievers come from? The very first golden retriever was originally bred in Scotland in the 19th century. More precisely, origins of this breed are associated with Glen Affric in the Highland region of Scotland. They were bred at the estate of the 1st Baron Tweedmouth, Dudley Marjoribanks.

Back then, hunting was a very popular sport or pastime for men across Europe. Parallel to the popularity of hunting the need for a more efficient retriever dog increased too. Hunters wanted a dog that was fast and good at retrieving but at the same time gentle enough to bring back the animal undamaged.

Dudley Marjoribanks acquired the only yellow puppy in a litter of black retrievers and named him Nous which means "wisdom" in Greek. A few years later, Nous was paired with a now extinct breed Tweed Water Spaniel, a female named Belle. Two dogs became parents to four yellow puppies, which marks the foundation of new golden retriever breed.

It would take a few decades for these cute dogs to gain public attention though. They remained unknown until 1904 when one of baron Marjoribank's dogs won the first field trial for retrievers. At the time, these dogs were registered with the Kennel Club of England as "retrievers – wavy or flat-coated." Four years later, in 1908, golden retrievers were shown for the first time in a class for "flat coats of any other color," and it would take five additional years, until 1913, for the breed to be recognized as yellow or golden retrievers.

In the early 1900s, golden retrievers were introduced to the United States, and they became popular immediately. No surprise there. The first golden retriever was registered with the American Kennel Club in 1925 while the Golden Retriever Club of America was established in 1938, which speaks volumes about the popularity of this breed. The rest is history; golden retrievers have become one of the most popular dog breeds, loyal pets, and beloved family members.

BREED INFORMATION AND BEHAVIOR

Golden retrievers are outgoing and trustworthy family dogs that are eager to please their owners. Compared to other breeds they are easier to train thanks to their loving and pleasing nature. This is going to be handy when you start the training process. As you've probably noticed already, golden retrievers are happy and joyful dogs that take a playful approach to life.

Even in adulthood, they maintain that puppyish behavior which makes us love them. Puppyish behavior isn't just about playfulness but the well-known innocence these dogs have. It's impossible not to love golden retrievers. Golden retrievers are energetic and love spending time playing outside.

Golden retrievers are mellow around children and nice to strangers and other animals. They require a significant amount of grooming and attention, but it's all worth it when they look at you with their big, dark eyes and huge grin on their face. Goldens are a big furball full of love. They are ideal for families, a quality nice to remember if you've just bought your first golden retriever or you're planning to do so.

Let's look at some of the most important characteristics of golden retrievers:

Friendliness

They can adjust to most living spaces as long as they get enough exercise and physical activity

Golden retrievers need about an hour of exercise a day

They are trainable and want to please their owners, so it's relatively easy to participate in all sorts of activities with them

Devoted and gentle

Although they are bred to be obedient and welcoming, goldens will still protect their owners whenever necessary

Golden retrievers shed a lot

Their fur is thick, silky, and beautiful, but it requires a lot of care

Goldens rarely bark. When doing so it's usually a welcoming or a friendly greeting

COSTS OF OWNING A GOLDEN RETRIEVER

Costs of owning a golden retriever vary and depend on your location, dog's needs, and other factors. Some services and products are cheaper in certain locations while others are more expensive. Generally speaking, the average costs are between $1350 and $1650 a year. This includes, at least:

- $300 for vet care
- $300 for grooming
- $500 for food and treats
- $250 for other expenses

Getting a golden retriever puppy may cost a little bit more during the first year because the little one needs a leash, crate, and other things, but it isn't necessary to buy them every month.

GROWTH AND DEVELOPMENT

Golden retrievers can grow up to be big dogs with amazing fur and a playful character that makes them the best friend a person could ever have. It's useful to get informed about their growth and development so you can plan their training, crate, and their own space accordingly.

The average height of an adult golden retriever is 22 inches while the weight is between 55 and 75 lbs.

Below, you can see growth and development charts for both males and females.

MALE GOLDEN RETRIEVERS

Age	Smallest weight	Largest weight	Average weight
7 weeks	3lb	17lb	9lb
8 weeks	5lb	17lb	10lb
9 weeks	8lb	17lb	12lb
10 weeks	10lb	22lb	15lb
11 weeks	12lb	25lb	17lb
3 months	16lb	43lb	22lb
4 months	25lb	44lb	30lb
5 months	27lb	57lb	40lb
6 months	29lb	72lb	44lb
7 months	32lb	77lb	48lb
8 months	40lb	85lb	55lb

FEMALE GOLDEN RETRIEVERS

Age	Smallest weight	Largest weight	Average weight
7 weeks	5lb	17lb	9lb
8 weeks	5lb	17lb	10lb
9 weeks	8lb	17lb	12lb
10 weeks	10lb	22lb	15lb

11 weeks	12lb	25lb	17lb
3 months	16lb	33lb	22lb
4 months	22lb	44lb	30lb
5 months	25lb	52lb	40lb
6 months	27lb	61lb	43lb
7 months	31lb	67lb	45lb
8 months	40lb	70lb	52lb

Now that you know more about golden retrievers, their history, temperament or nature, and growth, you're ready to learn more about training and are ready to start with a five-week schedule.

CHAPTER 2:

2:
THE MOST COMMON GOLDEN RETRIEVER TRAINING PROBLEMS

Although golden retrievers are obedient, and they love to please their owners, training should still be taken seriously. A common mistake that many owners repeat is that they think goldens don't need some specific strategy because they learn fast and do what their owners say anyway. The training schedule is always important, regardless of the breed. Before you start with a five-week schedule that will help you train your golden retriever puppy or adult dog, there's still a thing or two worth learning about the training process and other matters.

Trust me on this one, as a dog owner who's about to train a golden retriever you'll come across various problems or obstacles. When that happens it's easy to assume you're doing something wrong, it'll be impossible to improve, training is ruined, and you just don't have it in you. The more you focus on these negative thoughts, the worse it gets. Training is a complicated process, and although we'd like everything to go smoothly, there's going to be a few bumps on the road. It's perfectly natural! That doesn't mean you're doing a bad job, though.

In order to make the training process more successful, you need to be prepared for different types of behaviors and other obstacles that may occur. This chapter focuses on the most common problems that owners of golden retrievers face regarding training.

These problems can be about behavior, owners, and other things that you can easily avoid when you identify them.

THINKING YOU'RE TOO BUSY

By far the most common problem that dog owners face is the belief they don't have enough time to train their four-legged friend. Sure, modern lifestyle is busy and hectic. We work a lot and just want to go home to get some rest. Sometimes it feels our schedule just involves going to work, returning home, getting some sleep, and then repeating everything all over again. While a day may seem insufficient, it's more than enough when you're organized.

The reality is that you're not too busy to train your dog. You just haven't found the ideal timetable for that activity. So, take your planner; if you don't have one try writing down your weekly tasks on a piece of paper along with daily schedules. Then, analyze what you've written and determine the best time to train your dog based on your commitments, responsibilities, and the schedule itself. That way, you won't feel like there's no time and it's highly likely you'll stick to the process.

INCONSISTENCY

Lack of consistency often goes with the above-mentioned problem. Without an adequate schedule, it's difficult to be consistent, and your dog doesn't receive proper training. Inconsistency is bad for you as a dog owner as well. You're under constant stress to keep up with training, but at the same time you have other commitments too. That's why it's always better to determine when to train your dog and make sure training sessions are consistent. It's also important to mention that consistency is also manifested through effort and dedication to the schedule you'll see in this book.

LACK OF INTERVENTION

We love our dogs and consider them family, which is exactly why we often let some things slide. It's not uncommon for a dog to do something mischievous and we don't do anything about it because he's so fun and cute. One thing after another and the problem occurs because the dog believes such behavior is acceptable, so he's going to continue doing that. While some mischievous things may be cute and fun, you need to intervene and introduce a healthy and correct behavior in a positive manner. I've experienced this problem on more than one occasion. I'd let my pup do all sorts of things I considered "cute" only to have to correct them through training later on.

LACK OF CONFIDENCE

Dog training requires patience and a well-structured schedule, but it also relies greatly on a person's confidence. If you're not confident, it will show in the way you're training your dog and, as a result, the little one will not take you seriously. While you don't have to be a strict tyrant (and that's not recommended), you do need to show authority so that your dog will listen to you and perform commands you issue. Without confidence, you'll believe it's impossible to train your dog or that you're just wasting your time. That type of behavior is unhealthy for both involved parties. Now that you know this arm yourself with confidence, it'll show in the way you train your golden retriever.

OVER-STIMULATING YOUR DOG

Many people overexpose their dogs to various stimuli. However, when you overload the puppy (or even an adult dog), you may be setting a foundation for behavioral problems. Basically, your dog is overwhelmed with different stimuli and isn't sure how to respond to them. This has a negative impact on his mind and behavior. The most significant contributing factor to behavior problems in dogs is allowing them to have way too much outdoor access during puppyhood and juvenile years. The world seems like a huge place to them at that point, and it becomes tricky to control their behavior in the long-run. Overexposure to stimuli causes inappropriate behavior which you can change by controlling all access to a stimulus that leads to those actions until your dog is able to handle it responsibly on his or her own. Although it may seem like a perfectly normal thing to allow your puppy to play outside as much as he wants it can still make the little one stressed and frustrated, thus leading to behaviors like becoming too irritated indoors.

TRAINING TOO LONG

We have a certain deadline in our mind by which we expect the dog will be trained perfectly. In order to succeed in training by that day, we often train and practice over and over again. The whole process can be exhausting for your dog although you may not realize it. It's not all fun and games. Training too long can also make your dog feel bored, and he loses interest in commands and tricks. It's needless to mention you practically overload your dog with new information.

This can lead to a counterproductive effect where you don't achieve the desired goal, but only induce the formation of behavioral problems in your dog.

BEHAVIORAL PROBLEMS

Not all training-related problems are down to owners. It takes two to tango, right? A common issue comes in the form of behavioral problems in a dog. More precisely, some types of behavior are considered perfectly okay, and we don't pay attention to them enough to create a schedule to prevent those activities. Before we start with the training schedule, here are some common behavioral problems in dogs, See if you can recognize them in your own puppy (or adult dog):

- Digging
- Chewing
- Not coming when called
- Pulling on the leash
- Whining for attention
- Barking at the door
- Aggression
- Jumping up all the time

CHAPTER 3:

3:
THINGS TO KNOW BEFORE TRAINING YOUR DOG

In order to train your golden retriever successfully it's important to get educated about the breed and the characteristics that make your dog such a great pet, but a challenging training task at the same time. The incredible popularity of golden retrievers can sometimes prevent you from getting the most out of this experience. Why? It's simple. We think we know everything there is about golden retrievers and fail to absorb more information about these dogs. As a result, it's difficult to achieve desired results, particularly within five weeks. That's why this book not only helps you teach your dog proper behavior but also provides education and overall support you'll need. Let's look at a few simple things you need to bear in mind before you start training your golden retriever.

DON'T WAIT TOO LONG

You just adopted (or got from someone) a golden retriever puppy, and the last thing you want is to "bother" him with the training schedule. I've been there. Little fur ball was so cute I didn't want to start with serious things immediately, but that's not the best decision in the world. Waiting for the perfect time to train your dog is a mistake because when you think about it, there's always going to be something that will stop you.

Don't wait too long to train your dog. After all, a puppy's mind is like a blank piece of paper. How it's going to be written is all up to you. At such a young age a puppy's brain is like a sponge, it absorbs everything, and although he's stubborn and playful, it's relatively easy to train him.

(Photo credit: Pixabay)

EXERCISE IS IMPORTANT

Golden retrievers are energetic and love to play all the time. These dogs require a lot of exercise. As mentioned earlier, goldens can adapt to any living space as long as they get enough physical activity. Regular exercise is also important for their weight management. When inactive goldens are prone to weight gain which can result in numerous health problems. Make sure your golden retriever doesn't end up being a couch potato. That's not in his nature. These dogs were bred to help retrieve prey while hunting. They are active animals that become unhappy when they don't get much-needed exercise. It's needless to mention that if a golden doesn't get enough exercise, he may develop behavioral problems. This adds more stress to the training process because you aren't sure why he's not adopting simple commands, when in reality the dog just lacks physical activity that helps him behave properly.

PLAYFULNESS ISN'T A FLAW

Goldens aren't like other breeds which tend to mature as soon as they reach the second year of life. Instead, these dogs are playful even in adulthood. Sometimes their playfulness is misinterpreted as a flaw that you need to correct. Retrievers remain in puppy state of mind even in their mature years, and it's important to nourish that spirit. It all comes down to teaching your dog healthy and correct behaviors while trying to fix flaws. That way, your dog gets to stay playful but well-behaved at the same time.

THEY ARE INTELLIGENT

You know what they say; golden retriever is the smartest blonde. Intelligence is one of the many traits these wonderful dogs have. Since they're incredibly smart, golden retrievers tend to get bored easily. Besides physical activity, mental exercise is also important to them. These dogs love games and other forms of activities that stimulate not only their body but their mind as well. Make sure you keep this fact in mind when you're training your dog.

GOLDENS LOVE FOOD

Golden retrievers love food. Not just love, they adore it actually! These dogs have a big appetite, and they'll eat as long as you let them or fill their bowl. Even though this is a cute thing, because it's impossible not to love your dog so dedicated to eating his snacks, it can lead to weight gain. Make sure your training schedule includes commands that promote physical activity and encourage him to exercise. Monitor your dog's eating habits in order to promote healthy eating behavior which will help your dog control his appetite.

THEY CHEW A LOT

Chewing is on the list of the most common behavioral problems in dogs, particularly golden retrievers. These dogs were bred to retrieve, but they have a soft grip that doesn't destroy the animal during hunting. Their nature makes them prone to chewing. Your golden retriever is probably a chewer, and you have a bunch of shoes and items to show for it. Many owners believe chewing is something their dog will never overcome, but that's not correct. Proper training teaches your dog healthy behavior. At the same time, your dog understands boundaries and knows what's his and what doesn't belong to him. This is a great way to control chewing and make sure your shoes and furniture remain intact.

(Photo credit: Public domain pictures)

CHAPTER 4:

4:
THE ROLE OF POSITIVE REINFORCEMENT IN DOG TRAINING

Dog training is an important part of the little one's life, but it's also a marvelous opportunity for you to bond with him (or her). There is no "one size fits all" approach when it comes to dog training. Options are endless, but not all of them are equal. Some methods are popular, but ineffective. A common belief is that the dog will learn things faster when you introduce punishments or when acting like a tyrant with whom they can't mess. Wrong! While authority is needed, you also need to exhibit understanding, support, show love, and make the whole training process a positive experience. That's where positive reinforcement steps in. Since the subject of this book is to train your dog using positive reinforcement, it's crucial to address this dog training method and its benefits.

WHAT IS POSITIVE REINFORCEMENT?

Positive reinforcement is a popular term in psychology and involves the use of positive stimulus to modify behavior. This method can be used when trying to teach a child to abandon an unhealthy habit, to train dogs, and in many other applications too. Positive reinforcement focuses on the addition of reinforcing stimuli following a behavior that makes it more likely that the behavior will repeat again in the future. At that time, a favorable action or behavior and desired response strengthen thanks to the addition of a reward.

In dog training, rewards are snacks, but also a positive approach toward behavior changes.

In the dog training world reinforcement is sometimes used incorrectly to indicate punishment. That's not quite correct! Punishment carries nothing positive. It only instills fear in your dog, which can ultimately lead to unhealthy behaviors. Reinforcement is the opposite of punishment. It's something that enhances or increases healthy behaviors and favorable actions. Reinforcement can occur naturally in a dog, or it can be deliberately created by the owner. You create reinforcement through treats and encouragement, but a dog can experience it through positive vibes, emotions, and of course an opportunity to eat his favorite snack.

The whole purpose of positive reinforcement is that the more often you encourage certain behavior, the more likely your dog is to repeat it again. The best thing about this training method is that you can apply it to your puppy or adult dog.

Positive reinforcement in a dog can also occur when he accidentally does something which results in more food or other things he loves. For example, if a dog keeps jumping and pulling stuff from the kitchen counter and accidentally pulls food on the ground, positive reinforcement just happened. He takes it as a message that when he jumps next time, the same thing will happen. That's why dog owners need to prevent positive reinforcement as much as introduce it. You need to make sure the environment isn't distractive or that it won't lead to scenarios described in this paragraph.

It's important to mention that although food is the first thing that comes to mind when positive reinforcement is involved, the method can also include some activity your dog loves, access to the desired area, more exercise, or something else.

Positive vs. Negative Reinforcement

Reinforcement in dog training can be positive and negative. As seen above, positive reinforcement refers to adding positive stimulus to promote a certain behavior or activity. But what is negative reinforcement? Negative reinforcement means to take something away. "Something" depends on the trainer, in this case, you.

For example, a trainer may take away the dog's ball or a treat due to undesirable behavior. He may also take away the dog's opportunity to play with other dogs by putting him on a leash. Negative reinforcement may also involve taking away something that is scary or painful. For example, negative reinforcement is included in many gundog training programs in the USA. During this process, the trainer starts by applying pain in the form of toe hitch or ear pinch. Pain isn't scary or horrible, but unpleasant enough for the dog to dislike it. When a dog carries out the desired behavior the trainer takes away the pain.

Benefits of Positive Reinforcement

Yelling, shouting, expressing anger in any way won't help you train your dog, especially not within five weeks. Goldens are gentle creatures, and they don't really thrive in a negative environment. Positive reinforcement takes away punishment but introduces behavior changes in a healthier, more accepting manner. This method is becoming increasingly popular thanks to the numerous benefits it provides. Some of the most significant advantages of positive reinforcement are listed below:

- Establishes rituals and training actions incompatible with the negative behavior
- Lowers dog's anger and frustration
- Enables the dog to feel good
- Dog's trust in the owner isn't violated
- The improved bond between dog and his owner
- Provides affection
- Encourages cooperation
- Increases a dog's enjoyment of social interaction
- The dog becomes more tolerant, self-controlled, and behaves more predictably in different situations
- Improves the dog's confidence
- Keeps enthusiasm high

CHAPTER 5:

5:
WEEK 1 –
TRAINING STARTS HERE

Now that you know more about golden retrievers, the importance of positive reinforcement in dog training, and problems that you need to overcome while promoting certain behaviors, it's time to start training. As discussed already, it's important to establish a schedule and introduce consistency so that both you and your dog can benefit from this experience. Golden retrievers are easier to train than other breeds due to their obedient nature and desire to please their owners. In fact, you can train your dog in five weeks successfully by following the weekly schedule in this book.

Now you probably think there's no way you can do it in five weeks, and I thought the same thing when I was trying to train my golden retriever on my own. This exact schedule helped me train it in five weeks, and I was thrilled, so my goal is to help you achieve the same goal. Throughout this chapter, you'll see the things to do during the first week of training your golden retriever. Are you excited?

INTRODUCING THE CRATE

The crate is made of collapsible metal or, in some cases, plastic, and it's large enough for your dog to stand up and turn around. Some dog owners believe crates are cruel, but that's not correct. The truth is that crates satisfy the dog's instinct to be in a den. It's the one place in your home that belongs to a dog only, and he finds it comforting, especially times when you're not around. Many dog owners put toys and other stuff your dog likes into crates. The crate is the dog's bed and sanctuary; it provides safety, confinement, and security for the dog while preventing destructive behavior. The crate is the place where the dog goes to spend time when owners aren't around, and it plays an important role in the training process.

https://www.shutterstock.com/image-photo/dog-cage-isolated-background-happy-labrador-745331356?src=wI1P46Jr2GsagpSpZLLfMg-1-0

You won't start crate training your dog just yet. During the first week of dog training, you just need to introduce the crate to your dog. Start by setting up the crate at one specific place where your dog will spend his time. Take some time each day to let your dog inspect the crate in order to get used to it. Don't try to force your dog into it or attempt to train him. Just let your golden retriever get used to the idea of having the crate around so he can feel comfortable when the time comes to spend time inside.

Establishing a Routine

Golden retrievers, like other dogs, thrive on routine. Inconsistency bothers them, which is exactly why I keep repeating it. During the first week of training your dog, try to create a schedule that you'll follow for the next four weeks. Your dog's schedule should involve mealtime, playtime, walks, exercise, time for training. Strive to feed your dog every day at the same time, allow him to exercise or be physically active every day at the same time as well, and you know the drill. Ideally, you should stick to this routine even when the training period is over. This will help your dog to be comfortable, and prevents the development of some behavioral issues.

INVESTING IN TOYS

Puppies are like kids, and they need toys to have fun and stay happy. Now imagine golden retrievers and their puppyish character even in adulthood. Regardless of whether you're training a young or adult golden retriever, it's important to invest in toys during the first week of training. Get a variety of interesting toys that your dog will love. When buying toys try to opt for ones that provide mental stimulation too. Since golden retrievers are intelligent and need to keep their brain active, mentally stimulating toys are important to them. Buy different toys (mentally stimulating, cute, fun) and try to change them each week. That way, your dog has something new to play with every week, and he won't get bored so easily.

(Photo credit: Public domain pictures)

Sit

Does your golden retriever know how to sit on command? If not, this is the first command you need to train. Dogs tend to sit naturally, so it's simple to train them to do so, which is why this is something you need to complete in the first week of training. Your dog's favorite treats can be a positive reinforcement tool during this process. Set aside five to ten minutes each day during this week to work on this command with your dog.

First, you need to get the dog's attention by showing you have a treat in your hand. Then, hold the treat right above his nose, but not too high because your retriever might jump to get it. Move the treat toward his ears but make sure you're keeping it close to the dog's head. As soon as his rear lands on the ground say "good boy" or "yes" in a happy or an upbeat tone. Of course, this is when you need to give your dog his treat. Repeat the same process up to five times, i.e. until your dog sits at the sight of the treat above his nose. While holding the treat above your dog's nose say "sit." That way, he'll get used to the command and will sit when you say it even if the treat isn't in your hand. During the first week, practice this command regularly and continue to do so during "review" sessions in the upcoming weeks.

(Photo credit: Wikimedia Commons)

POTTY TRAINING OF YOUNG RETRIEVERS

If your dog isn't potty trained it's time to start doing so. Potty training can go hand in hand with crate training, and although we're not going to start with that in the first week, it's still useful to start with some potty-training measures. The most effective potty-training method is positive reinforcement. Crates are important for potty-training because dogs have a natural instinct to keep their den clean. Choose whether you want your dog to pee exclusively outside or not. Using potty pads and litter boxes can only slow down potty-training.

Make sure you avoid potty-training your dog outside, then inside, then outside again. This creates confusion and adds to inconsistency. Introduce potty training to his schedule and make sure you feed him regularly in order to predict and schedule bathroom breaks. Take the dog out for post-meal walks. During the initial stages of potty-training try to take your dog outside on an hourly basis. A great way to prevent "accidents" is to monitor the dog's behavior and notice changes that occur before "potty" time. Once you learn these changes, you'll know exactly when to take the dog outside. Always accompany the dog when taking him out, not only to ensure he'll really "go" but also to reward him for a job well done. You can use this same strategy to potty train puppies as well as adult dogs.

CHAPTER 6:

6:
WEEK 2 –
EASING INTO IT

The first week of golden retriever training is all about establishing a routine, introducing the crate, and getting toys your dog will use throughout the training process and beyond. Now that you've set the tone for a well-structured and effective training program let's pick up the pace and continue with the work we've already started. It's time to ease into the whole training thing and take it to a whole new level now. Here's exactly what to do during the second week.

DOWN AND EMERGENCY RECALL

Throughout the second week of golden retriever training spend a few minutes several times each day to teach your dog commands such as down and emergency recall. Teaching your dog to lie down on command is as easy as training him to sit. This is a basic command your dog should learn in the early stages of the training process.

Prepare his favorite treats and make sure you train him in a quiet area without distractions. One training session should last about five to ten minutes. Get the dog's attention by showing you have a treat in your hand and hold it in front of his nose. Start to move the treat toward the ground slowly. Give the dog his treat and pet him as soon as his elbows and hocks touch the ground. Make sure that you're using the treat to get him to lie down say "lie down" so that he can do the command even when there's no treat involved.

(Photo credit: Public domain pictures)

The emergency recall is a command that teaches your dog to come to you in urgent situations. It's an important command to teach your golden retriever even if he already comes when you call his name. Sometimes dogs ignore when they're being called. This is yet another easy command that your dog can adopt during the second week of training. First, you need to choose a word that you'll use to recall your dog in emergency situations. It should be a word that doesn't frequently come up in conversation. Choose a unique word you want, but make sure it's easy to remember.

Start in a small and quiet area and use treats that you'll give him whenever he comes after hearing that specific word. Once he easily does this "job" in a smaller area, start practicing in a bigger location and so on. It's very important to let your dog resume the activity he was doing before you used that word to call him. The reason is simple; some dogs refuse to come to their owners because they know their fun activity is about to come to an end. That's not what you want to achieve with emergency recall so always let him go back to what he was doing before.

Not to worry if your dog doesn't come when called. That's a command you'll be able to train your dog in week three.

CRATE TRAINING

In the previous week you introduced the crate to your dog, and by this time he has gotten used to the idea of having it around. The dog probably spent a few minutes there on his own without being taken there and left alone in the house, right? Now it's time to start crate training, which is important for potty-training and healthy behavior. Make sure crate training is positive, i.e. your golden retriever shouldn't consider crate time as some sort of punishment. Put something soft including toys in the crate to make it appealing and comfortable. Place some treats inside too. Don't force the dog inside, just let him explore it at his own pace. When he goes in on his own, say "good boy" and give him a treat.

Keep the crate door open until he seems comfortable and settled. Close the crate and let him stay for a minute. If the dog starts panicking, open the door and give him more time. Gradually increase the time of confinement in the crate but make sure you're there too. Start training him to be in a crate when you're not at home when he's used to the idea of being closed in a crate. The process is simple. Close the crate and leave the house for a minute. Go back, give him a treat. Gradually increase the time spent outside your home to train your dog to get used to you being at work for hours.

Make sure you reward favorable crate-related behaviors with treats.

LOOSE LEASH WALK

The second week of dog training is a great time to teach your dog to walk on a loose leash. It'll be easier for you to take your dog outside when he's trained to walk on a loose leash properly. Dogs tend to pull on a leash which can be frustrating to owners, but dangerous to dogs. For the purpose of training, you'll need a six-foot leash and a collar. Now, choose the command you'll give to your dog, so he knows what to do. You can use commands such as "let's go" or "with me." With a dog beside you, issue the command and start walking. As soon as the dog starts pulling the leash stop immediately. Make sure you don't move forward when he's pulling the leash.

The goal is to teach your dog that the only way for him to get where you are headed is by avoiding pulling, and as soon as there's some slack on the leash start walking again. Each time your dog pulls, stop. Give him the command and start again. Repeat the process until your dog learns leash walk, but make sure you're using treats to introduce the behavior you want. To get his attention and keep him relaxed while walking, give him his favorite treat.

Practice this regularly, especially when you're taking your dog outside to run or exercise in the park.

https://www.shutterstock.com/image-photo/owner-walking-golden-retriever-dog-together-357985871?src=jWbmF9etswxQvk5vBKLVbQ-1-1

CHAPTER 7:

7:
WEEK 3 –
TIME TO DO FUN THINGS

We've come a long way, and it is now time to tackle some fun training techniques to progress toward even more useful commands that you can teach your dog. In this section, we will cover three important commands that many people tend to struggle with, yet they are very important in terms of having a dog that is more obedient and a Golden Retriever that really listens to you

The three commands that we will be focusing on during the third week of our training is come, leave it, and stop jumping. All three of these are basically obedience training commands, but this does not mean they have to be boring. With some creativity, you can make learning each of these commands fun for both you and your dog, and you can get your dog to know what each of these terms means by the end of this week.

We'll start with the most basic one, getting your dog to come to you on command. This is important in many scenarios, but we often find that our dogs become distracted quickly and fail to obey this particular command. Once your dog starts to get more accustomed to the "come" command, we'll get your dog to understand when they are requested to leave something, and then, finally, we'll tackle a command that can get rid of a particularly annoying thing that many Golden Retrievers tend to do – which is to start jumping on you and your guests when they get too excited.

COME

Ah, the one command that so many new dog owners tend to struggle with. You take your dog on a walk through the park, decide to let him off his leash for a few minutes so that he can have a little freedom, and before you know it, your dog has his eyes set on a squirrel running around just a short distance from you. As your dog starts to run toward the squirrel, you start yelling to him, "COME!". Yet, he simply continues to run off and chases the squirrel.

This is only one example of many situations where you would want your dog to come to you. If he doesn't know what that command means, he is going to continue running off. One problem with a dog that doesn't understand what it means when you tell him to "come" is that failure to train him appropriately to understand this command could put his life in danger.

If your dog doesn't come to you when you use the recall command, then it is time to get to work.

To train your dog the recall command, you need to have already established a good and strong relationship with your Golden Retriever. You'll also need some treats that your dog enjoys a lot in order to teach him this command.

First of all, understand that the recall command, when you tell your dog to "come," should be associated with positivity – with rewards. Don't tell your dog to "come" and then scold him or put him in his crate. Additionally, if you have already used the term "come" a lot and your dog might have started to associate the term with something already – especially if this something is negative – then you will have to think of a different word to use for the recall command.

To teach your dog the come command, you should ask a friend or someone you trust to help you. It will be a good idea if your dog is also accustomed with the person that will be helping you out. You will start by using your dog's name, then introduce the recall command that you have decided on.

Start by sitting opposite each other, but make sure there is not too much distance between you and the person who is helping you out. You will start by calling your dog by its name, while your friend is restraining them. Get your dog to run to you when you call him by his name. Take turns doing this, until your dog gets comfortable – and remember a treat whenever he responds.

After a few times calling him by his name, switch to the specific recall command you decided on.

During the entire time, make sure the training session is fun for your dog. Never punish him for not obeying the recall command but be sure to reward him when he does obey.

This technique should be practiced repeatedly. Even when your dog listens to you every time you tell him to come, be sure to continue practicing ensuring he maintains the skill and will always continue to obey your recall command.

(Photo credit: Flickr)

LEAVE IT

Next up is another very useful command that you need to teach your dog, as part of obedience training – the "leave it" command. This one can also be hard to teach in some dogs but still serves an important purpose. You want your dog to listen to you when he starts to shred your pillows into pieces or gets into some valuable things, as well as when he starts to bite. The command is also useful when walking about, and your dog suddenly wants to catch a squirrel, similar to the usefulness of the recall command.

This command should also be taught in a fun way. Avoid punishing your dog if he fails to 'leave it' on command but be sure to adequately reward him if he does leave it when you give him the command.

You have to start out with the basics here, as expecting your dog to listen to the "leave it" command when he is off leash and has his eyes set on something really is unwise. Instead, start training him on-leash if possible and in the house. This will ensure you have more control over the environment and the situation.

It is a good idea to start by placing a treat underneath the front end of your shoe. Allow your Golden Retriever to notice the treat, but don't allow him full access to the treat. He may sniff it and even try to claw it out, but he should not be able to. Once he loses interest, reward him with a treat – but not the one that is underneath your shoe.

Add your preferred "leave it" command after he succeeds a couple of times. Then move on to letting a treat fall without your shoe on top. Tell your dog to leave it and reward good behavior and obedience. As you progress, you can start purposely planting a couple of distractions on your regular walking path and command your dog to "leave it." When your dog is accustomed with this new command, try it off-leash and see how things go.

(Photo credit: Max Pixel)

STOP JUMPING

The next one is important because it can become annoying. Think about those times when guests arrive at your house, and your dog continues to jump up onto them out of pure excitement. While this may seem cute as a puppy, remember that your Golden Retriever will become a relatively large dog – so jumping on someone can become a hazard.

To teach a dog to stop jumping up onto someone may take some time, so be patient here. Start by getting someone to help you out. They will hold the dog on his leash, and you will be taking advantage of the command "sit" here, which you previously taught your dog.

Get your friend to tell your dog to sit, then start to approach your dog. As you approach, he might get up – at this point, turn around and walk away. Your friend should tell your dog to sit again, and then you approach him once again. If you can get close to your dog without him getting up, it is time for a reward. Practice makes perfect, so continue doing this every day until your dog learns that jumping up is not a rewardable behavior.

https://www.shutterstock.com/image-photo/golden-retriever-jumping-catching-food-against-750797152?src=Ho-iwfDPddH2alF4wvUHTg-1-0

REVIEW PREVIOUSLY LEARNED TRICKS

We've covered many tricks and commands so far, and we have reached the end of week three. By now, your dog should be able to sit down, lie down, come to you when called, and even behave when guests arrive.

Before we continue, I highly recommend taking some time off to revisit some of the commands you have taught your dog in the past three weeks. Go through them one by one, and remember to keep a lot of treats handy, as you'll need to reward him for obeying your commands. If you find that your dog struggles with any of the commands you've covered thus far, then go back and revisit that specific command.

CHAPTER 8:

8:
WEEK 4 –
STILL A LOT MORE TO LEARN

We've reached week four, and it is time to pick up the pace. At the end of the previous week, we did a recall on the tricks we've taught over the past couple of weeks, and now it is time to get back to training. During the fourth week, we will focus on three more commands that your dog should start to understand, listen to, and, of course, obey. Here, we will look at how you can get your dog to wait on command, how to get them to go to their own 'special place,' such as their bed, and how to get your dog to drop something.

As with the other weeks, be sure that you allocate time this week as well and be patient while you are training your dog. Have treats ready to give your dog, which ultimately serve the purpose of letting him know that he has done something right.

WAIT

We'll start out with the wait command – a very, very useful command that you definitely want your dog to know and obey. The wait command is useful in many different scenarios. Think about what happens when you try to feed your dog, and he continuously tries to push himself into the bowl while you are serving up his food. There are other cases where the wait is needed as well, so this command will be extremely useful to you.

Make sure you have the other commands down before you try the wait command. You'll be relying on sit, along with wait here, in some cases. Your dog should also understand basic obedience commands in order to take things a step further with the wait command.

The wait command is something that you will be teaching your dog continuously. It needs to become part of your daily routine. When you walk out the door with your dog, whether it is to take him outside after a nap or to go for a walk, be sure to use the wait command before you go outside. Your dog should not be allowed to just run out the door without first sitting down and obeying your wait command.

The process of taking your dog outside can be used to your advantage here, while you are teaching them to wait. Get your dog to sit down in front of the door, and then tell them to wait. Open the door just a little bit and see what your dog does. If they get up and get ready to go outside without your lead, close the door and tell them to sit. Repeat the process until they actually wait and sit still even when you have opened the door.

Once your dog sits still and waits for your command, step outside and tell them to come.

At this time, many of the previous commands you have taught the dog come in handy. You use both sit and come when you start teaching your dog to wait.

You should do this every single time you take your dog outside.

In addition to practicing wait when you go out, another area where you can use this technique is when you are feeding your dog. As you prepare his food, ask him to sit down and wait. When you want to place his bowl on the floor, tell him to wait. If he rushes forward as you move down to the floor, move the bowl up and tell him to wait. Do this until he does not rush toward the bowl, but rather waits for you to put it down and give him an appropriate command to enjoy his food.

https://www.shutterstock.com/image-photo/golden-retriever-park-198298748?src=RmAOAboc-UFQA-MjZUOVog-1-21

GO TO YOUR PLACE

The next one is also very useful and can be used when your dog seems to be getting in the way, such as when you are preparing dinner, or maybe when you have a couple of guests over. You want your dog to know where his place is and where to go when you are busy and unable to attend to him for the time being.

Teaching your dog to go to his place can take a little while, and you should be able to get your dog to lie down with a command like "down" already. If your dog does not respond adequately to your "down" command, then go back and make sure he understands what it means when you tell him "down."

Once he knows what you want when you tell him to lie down, you can start training him on the "go to your place" command – start by determining the right command to use. You may choose to use the command "place," or perhaps something like "bed" instead.

The first step is to introduce him to "his place" as he may not yet know what or where you want him to consider his place to be.

Get a few treats and stand near his special place – this could be his bed, or perhaps a special rug that you want him to lie on in the lounge. It is a good idea to have something specific — so be sure to get something portable if you are going to use the command in different rooms. Call the command you have chosen and then lure your dog with a treat to the specific spot. When he enters the spot, praise, and reward. Let him get off the place and then repeat the process.

As he gets more comfortable, get him to lie down when he steps on his bed or the special place you are allocating to him during the training session.

Your dog will eventually start to lie down by himself when he enters this space. You'll only have to give him the "place" command, and he'll automatically do the "down" one himself, without the need for a second command from you. For now, however, be sure to give him that second command until he is better acquainted with this new command you are teaching him, and until he really understands what you want when you give him the command "place."

DROP IT

Let's say you take a walk through the park and your dog gets hold of something that might be poisonous to their digestive system or generally harmful to them. What do you do? In these cases, the "drop it" command can be a real lifesaver, ensuring your dog immediately drops what they have picked up, instead of swallowing it. Unfortunately, your dog won't respond to your command if they do not know what "drop it" means. The command is also useful when playing with your dog — you want him to go fetch and then drop the ball in your hands or in front of you.

This one is rather simple to teach, but don't expect your dog to start listening to the cue immediately.

Grab your dog's favorite toy and let him have at it. Give him a minute to play with the toy, and then start with the training routine. You need to implement this technique before he gets tired of playing with the toy, as he should want to play with the toy for best results.

As your dog plays with his toy, take a treat and keep it close to his nose, but don't let him have the toy. When he leaves the toy, reward him for leaving it. Continue doing this several times. Let him play with the toy again, hold the treat near his nose, let him leave the toy, and then give him his reward.

After a few successful tries, you can start adding the cue to the technique. Tell him to "drop it," then reward him with a treat if he drops the toy. You should say "drop it" with the treat close to his nose.

As your dog starts to obey the command, you should keep the treat further away from his nose gradually. Ultimately, your goal is to get him to respond to "drop it" without having to offer him a treat every time, but rather by simply praising him for his obedience.

CHAPTER 9:

9:
WEEK 5 –
Bringing The Training To An End

After a long four weeks of training, we finally reach the final phase of the training program – week five. Your dog now has some of the most important training commands "up his sleeve," but there is still some room to grow.

During week five, we'll focus on the last few training techniques that you should implement. While these are not as important as sit, lie down, place, fetch, and let's not forget drop it, they will most definitely come in handy on many occasions.

We'll start by looking at an easy technique that you can use to get your dog to stop barking, without having to yell at him. We'll also take a look at the "heel" command. Finally, we'll review the progress by setting up different types of random tricks in order to see how your dog did during the last five weeks and then address any problems that might still be lingering with the commands you have taught your Golden Retriever.

Stop Barking

Barking is something that a dog does. It's his way of communicating, and it allows him to alert his owner of the potential danger that might be lurking. Unfortunately, barking can get out of hand sometimes, and this needs to be kept under control. You certainly do not want your dog to wake you up in the middle of the night, or keep your neighbors awake all night long.

So, what are you to do about it? Well, the good news is, getting your dog to stop barking might be an easier task than you think it would be.

By now, your dog has learned a lot of new commands and training techniques in the past four weeks. This means that it will be a little easier to get him to obey the stop barking command, so you should not have too much trouble with this one – still, know that it could take a little time, so be patient and spend some time on this one as well.

Excessive barking is usually considered a behavioral problem in dogs, and you should not expect your dog to stop barking with just one day of training.

Firstly, never yell at your dog when he is barking. He'll most likely think that you are joining in on the barking and will continue to bark, perhaps even louder.

You need to try to remove any motivations that the dog may have to bark for now. Close your curtains if your dog goes to the window and barks at everyone walking by. Take him inside the house if he continues to bark at everyone outside.

Ignoring your dog while he is barking is another strategy that sometimes works. Don't give him rewards or attention when he is barking. He will think that this is appropriate behavior that you want him to exhibit. Only reward him when he stops barking.

You may also provide your dog with something to do when he starts to bark – this "something" should be distracting to reduce the chances of him barking. For example, if your dog barks, tell him to go to his place and then give him a toy. With a toy in his mouth, he will be less likely to bark.

HEEL

Dogs do not automatically know how you want them to walk with you when you go to the park or for a walk down the street. They may constantly be pulling their way forward and falling behind. The "heel" command is extremely useful for getting your dog to walk next to you, instead of constantly pulling on the leash, but it's not to be confused with the command "learning to walk with a loose leash" from the previous weeks.

This is considered a more advanced trick than some of the other ones on the list, which is why I decided to introduce you to strategies that you can use to teach your dog the heel command. Your dog should at least know how to come, stay, and to sit by now.

You should have some treats ready for this technique. Get your dog to sit next to you – preferably on your left-hand side. Once they sit down and they are calm, start to walk slowly and get them to walk with you. Keep a treat in front of them so that they continue to walk by your side. Reward them for walking next to you. If they start to fall behind or move in front of you, get them to sit down and repeat the process again.

As your dog gets used to this way of walking next to you, you can slowly start to introduce them to the command "heel" – only use this command while they are located next to you, and give them a treat when you give the cue.

When your dog seems to be following the command appropriately, you can start to walk with him without holding a treat in front of him to follow around. See if your dog will stay next to you with the command "heel," and without a treat to constantly follow. If it doesn't seem to work, go back to the previous step, get him to follow the treat, reward good behavior, call out "heel" when he does well, and then try again without the treat.

PICK A TRICK

Congratulations for getting this far. During the past five weeks, you've spent a lot of time with your Golden Retriever, getting him to learn some important commands, with the ultimate goal of having a smart and obedient dog. If you have gotten all the tricks down, then now is the time to recap. Your dog has had a busy five weeks, and they may sometimes forget some of the commands that they were taught – there was a lot to learn, after all.

So, with "Pick A Trick," you will choose a random command that we've covered during the past five weeks and see how your dog responds to a random verbal cue that you call out. Try to think of one that he easily followed. Call out the cue and see how your dog responds. Remember to reward him with praise and, of course, don't forget a treat, if he follows the command through. Try to call out the commands that seemed a little harder for your dog as well. See if he can still remember them and implement them on command.

(Photo credit: Wikimedia Commons)

REVIEW

Get out a pen and paper or open up a notes app on your phone. Make a list of any commands that your dog seems to have forgotten or still seems to struggle with after the five-week training program is completed.

Once you have gone through all the commands that we covered and made a list, go through them one-by-one. Revisit the sections in my book that explains the techniques you should use to teach your dog each of the tricks he is having difficulty with. Take some time to focus on each of these until he seems to get it.

When you have gone through the list, take things from the top again. Give him random commands and see how he responds.

This might take some time, but return to any tricks he seems to be having difficulty with every time.

CHAPTER 10:

10:
COOL TRICKS TO TEACH YOUR DOG

Now that you have the basics done and your dog knows how to sit, stay, to go to his place, to come to you, and other important commands that you will rely on when you take him for a walk, you may be wondering what's next.

Luckily, training doesn't stop here. Once your dog can perfectly obey each of the commands in this book, you can still continue to teach him many cool, interesting, and smart tricks. Tricks can be more advanced in many cases and often takes more time. This is why it is important first to undergo basic training and follow through the five-week training program that I introduced you to here.

When your dog is more accustomed to training through the first five weeks, he will be easier to train further on. You'll find that teaching him new tricks become much easier when he knows how to obey the more basic commands.

There are quite a large number of tricks that you can now start teaching your dog. As with the previous ones that we covered, always be patient with your dog and understand that he is not going to get this right the first time you try it. Many of the more advanced tricks also take multiple steps. You'll have to start at step one and wait until your dog is able to follow the first step, then proceed to step two, and move forth in such a way.

I highly recommend you start with a basic trick like "shake hands" or "give paw." This is one of the easier advanced tricks you can teach your dog. It is simple enough to help you get started with a few tricks but will still take some time. I would suggest at least a week to teach your dog this trick before you proceed to another one. Give your dog an entire week to learn a new trick – and only move on to the next trick when your dog is able to do exactly what he needs to do in order to achieve the 'trick' that you have taught him.

Other cool tricks that you might also want to consider include:

- Spin
- Play dead
- Speak
- Kiss
- Roll over

CHAPTER 11:

11:
MISTAKES TO AVOID WHEN TRAINING YOUR DOG

Before we conclude with this training program, I want us to cover one more topic. I have seen a lot of dog training books miss out on this section – I'm referring to a specific section on mistakes that need to be avoided when you are trying to train your dog. Unfortunately, many trainers only focus on telling you what to do when you train a dog, and they forget how important it is to tell a new dog owner what they should not do.

I have found that new dog owners tend to make a lot of mistakes when they are trying to get their dog to learn commands and tricks. This often leads to problems. The dog starts to disobey orders or simply does not train well at all. These can all be avoided by educating yourself on what mistakes are common among new dog owners, and how these mistakes can be effectively avoided to yield better results when you get to the point when you want to start implementing a training program for your dog.

If you continue to make mistakes during your training session with your Golden Retriever, both of you will end up being frustrated with the other. This will not lead to time well spent, but rather to complications that will make training harder for both you and your dog.

Firstly, I need you to understand that your body is able to read your body language and understand what you are going through. If they can sense that you are frustrated, they will become frustrated too.

Don't start to yell at your dog when he gets frustrated or when you feel angry at him. He will not understand you – remember that he doesn't speak English and you have to teach him to obey specific commands that you want him to understand. Yelling at him will only aggravate the existing problem and make things much worse than it already is.

Instead, be calm. This is one of the most common mistakes that new dog owners make when they try to train their dog. They get frustrated, become angry, and they start to yell at their dog. Believe me, you're not going to achieve anything with this sort of behavior. When you are calm, you have a better chance of calming your dog down.

Now, apart from not staying calm and starting to yell, there are other mistakes that you might also be guilty of – often without knowing it. Let's explore some other common mistakes in terms of dog training that you need to avoid.

COMMAND POISONING

This one is quite common. As soon as you get your dog to obey certain commands, you start using these commands frequently during the day. The problem is, with positive reinforcement training, your dog is not going to continue obeying a specific command if he starts to associate it with something negative. Let's say you ask your dog to come and then give him a treat. He associates the command with something positive, and he learns it. After a few training sessions, he will gladly come to you when called with a recall command.

A few days in and you recall your dog but follow his action with something negative. Perhaps you punish him after he comes to you. Maybe you give him a bath. This creates a negative association with the command for the dog – do you really think his going to continue coming to you when called if he thinks he will be going for a bath? No!

Only associate the commands you teach your Golden Retriever with positive things, like treats, praising, and other things that they enjoy.

NAGGING AND NAGGING, AND NAGGING

You hate it when someone keeps nagging you for something, so why should your dog enjoy you nagging him? Nagging is something that I have also seen a lot of people do – and this is a really bad habit that you need to avoid from the start!

What do I mean by nagging? How many times do you call your dog before he comes to you? If he doesn't come right after the first time, and you have to repeat the command several times, you are nagging. He might eventually come to you – but what you have just taught your dog is that he is allowed to wait until the fifth, sixth, or maybe even the tenth from a specific command before he has to comply.

You obviously want your dog to respond to your commands immediately – so do NOT nag with a single command. Instead, if you call him and he doesn't obey, see why he is distracted, get his attention, and then repeat the command without making him feel like you are nagging or that he has to wait for you to repeat a command several times before obeying.

Repeating Training Techniques That Don't Seem to Be Working

This is yet another one that many dog owners are guilty of – trying to repeat the same technique to get a dog to learn a specific command over and over, even when it becomes obvious that the technique they are using isn't working.

There are many ways that you can teach a dog a specific type of command. Come, stay, sit, your place – all these commands, and the other ones that we have gone through in this book, can all be adjusted to different scenarios.

Try a specific technique, and if you see that your dog isn't picking up on what you are trying to get them to learn, wait a while and try again. If it still doesn't work, then you need to take a closer look at the technique and try to make some adjustments in order to comply with what your dog feels more comfortable with.

It might take a few adjustments before you find a specific setting that allows your Golden Retriever to really get the hang of a specific command that you would like to teach them. Even when it seems like he is not obeying any of the commands you are trying to teach him, don't give up. Adjust and adjust again if necessary – you will get to a point where he listens and obeys.

CONCLUSION

The Golden Retriever is a great dog breed. They are used as family dogs and service dogs, and they are also excellent companions in a search and rescue party. For me, blue was the perfect friend, pet, and even a family member. From their floppy ears to their furry coat, there really is nothing I dislike about these dogs. The Golden Retriever is a very smart and lovable dog, and they really are easy to train – but only if you know what you are doing.

The most important part of training your Golden Retriever should be to have patience and take things one step at a time. When you try to rush things and jump from one trick to another, you are going to confuse your dog, and this will lead to no results – or maybe even a dog that becomes hard to train.

Unfortunately, many people think that their dog is too old to train, but I have some news for you – after reading this book, you should now understand that it is never too late to start training your Golden Retriever. While it certainly is beneficial to start training these dogs while they are still very young, life is often too busy to attend to a strict training schedule, and let's face it – they grow up so fast! No matter how old your Golden Retriever, you can still train them effectively and teach them a trick or two (or more).

In this book, you discovered everything that you need, and I have provided you with all the tools required to get started with a training schedule. The secret "ingredient" to successful training is to take action, not delay and, be persistent. Expecting your dog to remember something you've tried to train them once or twice is ridiculous. You need to take time out of your day – every day – and implement the training techniques that I have guided you through in this book.

Don't skip anything. Take things step-by-step. Start at week one and then work your way through the five weeks. When it seems like the progress you have made is declining, take a step back. Revisit some of the older tricks and training techniques that your dog seems to be forgetting, then implement these training methods again.

Remember that it will take some time and your dog will not be able to get every method down perfectly the first try. You will need to be very patient, and you'll have to stay calm, even when it seems like you are unable to make any progress. When you get upset and start yelling at your dog, it will make things worse, not better. Keep this in mind while you are going through the week-by-week training strategies. Your dog is able to read your body language, so be calm and collected, and in control.

The last thing – remember to have fun with your dog while you are training him/her. This is a great way for the two of you to bond and spend some quality time together!

Hey! How are you Dog Lovers? I hope you enjoy the contents that I have put all my heart and soul into so far! now, I just wanted to say thank you very much to support the book and our community. I know you're here because you're interested in training and raising your beloved dog. And just because Of that I have the gift for you! **receive your "For the Love of Dogs" Book. Which sells for 4.36 Dollars in store, but**

we give you for FREE! By simply enter the link: http://eepurl.com/dOxyd1

Just like what we have talked through the book **Treat Your Family with Love!**

Help to support the small writer and our dog training community, by Leaving us Reviews!

And If you want to be a part of us Please feel free to join our Facebook dog training Community (Dog Training made easy by David) by typing the link below.

fb.me/Dogtrainingmadeeasybydave

Thank you very much for your Support!

Best Regards,

Dave Peterson